The Way Back To Myself

A little more sunshine, where the heart smiles.

Manya Agarwal

India | USA | UK

Copyright © Manya Agarwal
All Rights Reserved.

This book has been self-published with all reasonable efforts taken to make the material error-free by the author. No part of this book shall be used, reproduced in any manner whatsoever without written permission from the author, except in the case of brief quotations embodied in critical articles and reviews.

The Author of this book is solely responsible and liable for its content including but not limited to the views, representations, descriptions, statements, information, opinions, and references ["Content"]. The Content of this book shall not constitute or be construed or deemed to reflect the opinion or expression of the Publisher or Editor. Neither the Publisher nor Editor endorse or approve the Content of this book or guarantee the reliability, accuracy, or completeness of the Content published herein and do not make any representations or warranties of any kind, express or implied, including but not limited to the implied warranties of merchantability, fitness for a particular purpose.

The Publisher and Editor shall not be liable whatsoever...

Made with ❤ on the BookLeaf Publishing Platform
www.bookleafpub.in
www.bookleafpub.com

Dedication

Dedicated to you. Yes, *you* — the one who understands what it means to feel too much. If you have ever fought to salvage something beautiful from a ruin, or simply needed permission to exist exactly as you are, this piece of my soul is yours.

To the hearts that have broken,
To the minds that have wandered,
To the drops that dared to fall,
And to every soul learning to love itself again!

Preface

These poems are pieces of my soul; the echoes of
unspoken thoughts, midnight realizations, and the silent
conversations I've had with myself.
Each poem here is a piece of that rhythm - sometimes
trembling, sometimes fierce, but always true.

These verses speak of self-love that grew out of cracks, of
a mind that wandered between chaos and calm, and of
small things that felt big...from breaking to blooming,
from losing to finding, from simply existing to feeling
alive again. And crucially, it is the story of the heart that,
having been broken, decides it will not simply survive,
but will live to love itself.

Some poems heal, some question, and some simply exist
— just as we all do.

If you've ever felt too much, loved too deeply, or tried to
make peace with your own reflection — these words are
for you.
If these words make you pause, smile, or feel seen —

even for a moment - then the purpose of this book is complete.

Because in every poem, there lives a piece of you too.

Acknowledgements

My deepest gratitude goes inward: to the struggling mind that wrote these words, and the heart that chose to heal itself. To life itself — for its storms and stillness, for teaching me that love, in every form, always finds its way back home.

To every soul who stood beside me — in silence, in chaos, in faith, whose love is the shore, constant and true. You gave me the space to whisper these feelings onto the page, and the strength to stand whole in the morning light.

To my readers — the feelers, the dreamers, the ones who search for light in their own shadows — this journey is as much yours as it is mine.

"The heart insists on thanking its shadows; they taught the self to bloom.
To the you: may these words be the home you were searching for in every room."

Happy Reading... :)

1. Whispers from the Island

Those are the things that keep me going
Feels like I am the hero of my best coming
Something new has started, best of all
Looking through each window pane, I love it all.

The stairs were built again,
And I'm surely going to win the game.
Like on the island I am
No such things to bother at,
Just me and the thoughts
Which built me who I am.

Love the way I am today
Free from everything today
What I am today!
It's the best of mine, today.

Flowing like a river
Reflected in a mirror
I still see myself hung at a doorstep

Feels like the right step

Am I the only person, who's happy by her own, looking herself and smiling?
Maybe yes, maybe no
Am I the person who has now known how to live a life
Alone, just me and my thoughts, still dreaming of the island -
A beautiful island full of my thoughts and myself

Truly, a person changed...

2. Have I lost myself?

Deep in the sea I see myself,
To find the busy myself
I still ponder, will I get myself?

Maybe, tough seems though...I know it's not the end of the show
It's more to come, more to grow!

Will I be able to come back?
Or will it give me a tight pack...

Through all the milestones I try,
Still the same I cry!
Watching the sun, the moon and sky,
Still the same I cry!

Are there people around?
Hundreds I see, none I feel....
Can I ask the same question to myself?
Have I lost myself?

3. The last flower

Like those petals I fell…
Got flew by the winds,
Not surely landed well
Petals turned in scents, by the kings…

Dried ones are now left,
Still, are fascinated by the people
The petal battled till last
Who still remembers it's past?

The punch pink was perfect for it
Gradually turned in pebble black by the hit!

The flower's incomplete now
Now, who'll say wow?
That's not the end…
The growth is progressive
The bud is appearing
Though missing that feeling…

4. There's a way!

I don't like how the things change
Do we really need to make them?
Why they don't interchange..?
Sad there are more & more to defame.

The colour of the wall reminds me of the spring
Can you let those memories bring..
Sun's shining to the fullest
But are the rays reaching?

Look! Standing and laughing are the leaves,
While the exquisite flower is broken to pieces...
The new flower is yet to germinate
Oh leaf, you'll forever terminate.

Deep is the sense,
Kind is the heart,
Pure is the mind,
Gentle is the spirit.

Things do change, takes a little while.
Good is the way, next with the best mile.

....

5. Wave?

The imprints are embedded hard
Like those of the foot on the sand
Sand so quiet…bearing the foot happily,
Will a light wave be shattering?

Peacefully it has accepted.
Is that right?
The cruelty. The fear. The pain.

Waiting for the right strong wave, as on the beach I wait.
Till that time, I happily discover seas.
The washing imprints give pain,
The separation is tough and rough,
But having it makes feel enough.

The dawn of the day will say it all
The sand will say about itself, no imprints will rule.
The strong wave says it all!

6. Lost

Isn't this too fast?
Like yesterday was summer and today it's winter..

The eyes are wet, chasing the dream set,
I wish the old would come again, making the memories relive once again!

The morning is set,
I wish I could go back through the same jet,
The hut is waiting...
Wondering and just wondering!

The world is colourful,
But why everything looks so dull?

Strengthening, handling each day
Is there a ray?

Eyes closed, the world stops
Rushes back to old and gold...

Moment the brain actives,
So the moments drain..

I wish I could run back
Asking the same again and again..
Isn't this too fast?
Or the world's vast..?

7. They Sky

The sky held high
Holding the stars much by.

I still wonder how the days pass,
With the growing dull grass.
Hoping the moon could shine again,
Crossing the bloody vein.

The moments were true
which held the the whole crew...
Wishing that would be real
Making it the most fiel.

Since the moon has faded away,
Everything seems so grey...

Limits myself to the most of myself,
What if I become the least of myself?

The sky still held high,

Pouring the rain to make me shy.
The vapours are casual, the cloud's constant...
Waiting for that rainbow to appear
Such that my thoughts are mere..

8. It forms a part of us

It forms a part of us
Creating out a huge fuss

The drops on the dull surface
Leaves no trace...

Being alone doesn't matter right?
The nature forms the back
Paper down there makes me right...
Motivation is what...I miss right.

Ironically it's arduous...or really it is?
I'm jubilant to it...are you?
Parting the way, following the ray!
Everything seems to be alright, is it the way?

It forms a part of us
Carrying it around not with a curse
Creating out a huge fuss
Does it really forms a part of us?

9. A Gem

You're a gem
Clouds cannot wave you off.

Gems are rare
So you are

The heart is light, yet so pure..
Is forgiving the only cure?
Trying to value the worth, until its dark avenue
Waiting in the queue,
It's the god, always with you...

Overcoming the fear of losing
Yet another lesson of self respecting

Tears in rain make it more soothing
Moreover, should I stop bothering?

The depressed mind is now tired
Can the new ties be wired?

The question's with God, humans are stupid when God's actions are guided!

10. When Everyone Leaves

The day was fine...the wind was blowing
Suddenly the time swaps, everyone going

The darkness appeared...
Phases were weird

Looking each corner, just to find silence
Finding peace isn't just too intense?
I still wonder am I alone?
Or is it everyone's a clown..?

Trapped inside wholly...
There's no one with you at the end, merely the holy

Everyone leaves, the soul and mind is one self's,
How one could arrange everything in one shelf?

Wondering, accepting; the world's cruel!!
Mattering the most is the 'moral'

'End this up' is just too easy
Postponing this...making me lazy

Trying to be myself
But dependence is all hard thyself!

11. A confused state

The day it began, gave me terror.
The butterflies stopped, water stood still.

I remember those days how beautiful they were
Wish I could gain them again and wear.

Is it becoming a burden?
Who knows the answer It's just me and the mind striving to conquer...
Give me some strength to handle everything;
Just left with new books and nothing
Can we let those books come in again?

It's not a question anymore....
Just struggling to do more and more.
Wish God is guiding me right
But, what if mind is making me fight?

Still in a confused state, will I get a better estate?

12. Down the lane

What calls you here?
The light in you or the spark?

Getting down at one thing again and again,
Is that me down the lane...

Distracting me from the path I wanted
Is that really a thing to get worried?

Simplifying things and thoughts
Still they mingle and tangle a lot!!

Fighting those away,
Remembering every day,
Still in the same play,
Proving each day.

The experiences drag upwards,
But then the mind force me downwards.

Listening to everyone and understanding everything,
Many ideas affect me, but I am dreaming...

Questioning again, is that me down the lane?

13. Is the moon lying?

Is the moon lying?
Or is the moon loving?
The sky stands still, the stars watching
But still, the moon's standing...waiting
The night comes, the night goes, moon is still waiting.

Listening to the stars singing,
watching the owls staring moon fades.
...the sun shines.

Is that the story getting over?
Or the new story begins.
A new night comes excitingly
The moon rules lovingly.

The end will never come.
So does the moon will never stop....
The moon's loving, waiting...
Still, is the moon lying?

14. The silent scream

Unheard to many, the screams are silent.

I don't like this
This patriarchy sucks..
I hate how 'they' rule everything
Isn't it wrong? The way, the gestures, the words.

The slight whispering is forbidden
The heavy laughs are to be permissible.
The huge, the giant, the big is the king!
There's no queen: many kingdoms, with no queens.

I still wonder they'll fall, to the ground, to the hell,
For 'her' to fly in the high sky.
I still wonder her eyes will roar, her actions will prove.
Just wonder.

Years on years, things remain same.
Unheard to many, the screams still remain silent.

15. The Truth's bitter

Feels like that was yesterday...
I count from Monday to Sunday
Not even a day passes by...which made me cry

Am I the strong one? Or that's making me more weak..
Feels like a small adjusted creek !

The new mountains broke the inner self
The mountains attracted, submerging the brook...
The brook floats and floats...finding new ways...
While the brook forget the mountain grey?

The snow will shed,
Slowly brown will head...

True images pertain fast,
Imagining how long the promise last?
The new mountain collapsed,
Still the brook floats with the old
Old & old...just together!

The brook was the constant
Coming of variables, breaks the constant...
She fought till the end, aiming the victory
....With the heavy injury

16. The dark life

The sunshine slightly passes the clouds,
The deep ocean still waits for the exotic light
All same for the mere ocean - day & night.
Though sand, Yes! Waiting long to have the moulds.

The stars shine, the waves flow
In the silent deep – angler makes a glow!

The breeze whispers tales unknown,
Of journeys begun, yet never shown.
The ocean sighs — it knows the lore,
Of dreams that fade, yet rise once more.

The bright morning, a tiny coconut grows
Dead are those fishes on the shore,
The small heart wanted some more –
Is there any cure?

17. Drop

In the midst of the clouds,
Lives a tiny drop –
Urging to pour hard
Trying to reverse the cards

Countering the dark agony & vexation,
Nobody's adhering to the blue's cumbersome.

A tab completes the jigsaw puzzle,
A lake can be full, with a drizzle?

Oh dear drop! Brimmed with passion
Urging to build a mansion,
Waived by the wave –
No more alive – a tiny drop

In the midst of the clouds,
Once lived a tiny drop.

18. The boat

The mind is tiring, losing the originality
Yet the rain making feel so soothing...

The blue sky is all the hope,
The still boats still make the lake spoke.

The storming rain, the precarious waves...
You are the warrior my boat!

No shelter no warmth, yet a happy place for another tenth.

You are still at the place my boat...
Being yourself is all you, helps just a coat.

The winds may test, the tides may bend,
Yet your spirit knows no end.
Sailing through the dusk and dawn,
You teach — even alone, we move on.

19. Round & Round

Hey you, looking here
Up to the sky and back,
Your imaginations never let you come back.

You find people
That continue the story's prequel.

But let me tell you —
Round and round the prequel dances,
And leaves you with same glances.

You chase the stars, yet miss the spark,
The mirror within still stays dark.

Every glance feels déjà vu,
New faces, yet the same old hue.

The story spins, the pages blur,
And still you wonder — who you were.

The echoes fade, but thoughts remain,
A gentle joy, wrapped in quiet pain.

You walk ahead, yet turn behind,
Still searching for the peace of mind.

20. Light and flight

I wanna be a light like you
You wanna be some tight like me!

Make it all happen like… to the moon to the sky
May I get all happiness like those of fly.
Reaching sky, reaching moon
Reaching till that last noon, reaching the target soon…

Drop it dear, what you'll get,
with just a fight with deer.

The world's too wide to fear, my peer,
Chase the glow, not the tear.

Maybe it's not the win, but the way,
That paints the light of every day.

Drop it dear, what you'll get,
with just a fight with deer.

21. Rising Through Shadows

Dreaming of the best,
Which could build my nest
Passing or failing through every test,
Still I become the best!

Thoughts provoke me to say it
What will I get it?
The girl's standing, thinking
Don't move a step just rhyming...

Getting down at one thing again and again,
Is that me down the lane...
The bottle's still filled, the lights shin bright, am I going
towards the right?...
yes I am.

Leave it all, move alone
Everyone has gone
So is my chance now..!!

22. Ferris wheel

Up I go, the world turns small,
Wind in my hair, I feel it all.
The first rise, heart skips a beat,
A tiny thrill, a little sweet.

Round we turn, the highs and lows,
Life spins fast, and no one knows.
At the top, the sky feels near,
At the bottom, laughter and cheer.

Hold on tight, let go a little,
Every drop makes the ride more brittle.
The sun will shine, the rain may fall,
But every spin, I embrace it all.

Round and round, the Ferris Wheel,
A simple joy, a simple thrill.
Ups and downs, they come, they go,
Yet in this ride, I love the flow.

23. Snow

Cool and white it stands,
Softly covering the lands.

Whispers of peace in the air,
A calm so pure, beyond compare.

Each flake a dream, a fleeting art,
Melting gently, yet touching the heart.

Beneath its veil, the world seems still,
Hiding chaos with a gentle will.

Children laugh, their footprints show,
Moments frozen, hearts aglow.

When sunlight kisses, it fades away,
Yet leaves behind — a brighter day.

24. Nights

The late night... rain dripping
The tired body and mind thinking

Enlightened by the green sites...
Heavy mind has some - peaceful sighs!

Smile has its own meaning...
Are eyes are the one getting..?

Surrounded by some true souls,
It's true; mango is the king of the set fruit bowl...or should I say the Queen own?

Elegancy has its own aura,
Let's take the example of rather aurora?

Chloro leaves are shining right,
However, dim are the lights.
The spark will be visible soon...
Beautiful of all is perfectly perfect moon!

25. I, Yet to Begin

I have the potential, still I don't do that....
What is the reason, where am I lacking?...
Seeking a challenging task,
Trying to unwrap the mask.
I am still and will be on the peak, but a fear struck my mind,
Will I be still sitting under the tree teak?

How good those days were, no tension, no issues,
Just wiping the mouth with tissues.

Starting something new from today, I hope every day is my day....
Is there anyone with me, Yes probably lot...right WE?

Now the sun is rising, the wind feels near,
Whispering softly — "let go of fear."
The road may twist, but I'll still try,
For dreams don't grow unless they fly.

26. Maybe WE

Maybe we were never meant to race,
Just to walk together, at our own pace.

Maybe we spoke through silent eyes,
Dreaming beneath the same vast skies.
Maybe we stumbled, maybe we fell,
Yet carried stories only time could tell.

Maybe we tried, not to win or lose,
But to learn the paths we choose.

Maybe we grew in our own way,
Becoming better with each day.
Maybe it's not about holding tight,
But moving on with hearts still light.

Maybe we're threads in life's grand art,
Different colors, yet one start.
For through the storms and skies of grey,
Maybe *we* just found our way.

27. The Yellow flower

In the corner of the field it grew,
Beneath the sky of endless blue.

Not the tallest, not the rare,
Yet it bloomed with quiet care.
When I see that yellow hue,
I see both life and love anew.

They're not about the grandest show,
But growing, even when winds blow.

And though the seasons fade away,
Its colour whispers day by day...
That love, like flowers, pure and true,
Lives in hearts — and not in view.

Love that grows without a claim,
No show, no rush, no worldly fame.
Just two hearts learning how to be,
Rooted deep, yet wild and free.

28. In My Wonderland

Imagine you are in wonderland,
Relaxing like the desert's sand.

No nothing to worry or think,
Just living to eat and blink.

No one's to disturb you,
Just you and the sky blue.

What would those days be like,
Like the solid, pure ice.

Time would pause, the winds would hum,
A melody of peace would come.

The heart would rest, the mind would stay,
In a world where dreams don't fade away.

No rush, no race, no heavy sound,
Just stillness singing all around.

29. Seeking the Peace

I walk through days so loud, so fast,
Chasing moments that never last.

Smiles around, yet minds confined,
A thousand thoughts within one mind.

The world keeps spinning, I lose my way,
Dreams fade softly into grey.

Still I whisper, beneath the din,
"Where does true peace begin?"

Maybe it's not in mountain air,
Nor in places still and rare.

Maybe peace is something small,
A silent voice that hears it all.

It's in the breath between each thought,
In battles faced and lessons taught.

Not found, but felt — a gentle release,
The heart's own art of seeking peace.

30. Finding the way

The road was long, the signs unclear,
Each turn whispered, "not yet here."

I stumbled once, then once again,
Through joy, through doubt, through silent pain.

The stars were dim, the nights were wide,
I walked with hope as my only guide.

The map I had began to fade,
But strength was born from what I made.

For every fall taught where to stand,
And every loss — a helping hand.

Finding the way was never apart...
It lived right here, within my heart.

31. The fiery agony

It burns within, a silent flame,
No one to point, no one to blame.

A war inside the heart and head,
Between the words I left unsaid.

There are nights when it feels like the world is asleep,
And I alone am awake, watching the ceiling breathe,

It's strange how pain never screams out loud,
It just sits, somewhere between the ribs and the throat,

Each tear that falls, each breath I keep,
Is fire that wakes what once was deep.

It hurts, it scars, it tests my will,
Yet through the pain; I'm standing still.

For agony, fierce as it may seem,
Can spark the strength behind a dream.

And when the fire begins to cease,
It leaves behind — the light of peace.

32. Love the Way I Am

I've walked through seasons trying to change myself;
to fit into frames that others drew,
to wear smiles that weren't mine,
to speak softly when my voice wanted to rise,
and to hide the cracks that made me whole.

Perfection called, I chased its name,
Till I found peace in being the same.

Not flawless, no - but true and clear,
To stand with strength, not doubt or fear.

I speak with calm, I act with aim,
I hold my ground, I play my game.

No borrowed shine, no borrowed plan
Just pride within...

I love the way I am.

33. The golden hour

When the sun leans low, and the sky turns gold,
The world feels softer, stories unfold.

Shadows stretch, yet light remains,
A fleeting calm that breaks the chains.

It's the hour between day and night,
When silence glows, and hearts feel light.

The rush subsides, the noise takes rest,
The world exhaling, doing its best.

Each ray a whisper, gentle, pure,
Reminding us - what we endure.

In golden light, we learn to see,
How peace can shine so quietly.

For every ending holds its power,
And hope is born - in the golden hour.

34. A Leaf

It began as a whisper - unseen, unknown,
A tender spark where life had grown.

Reaching out to touch the sky,
With dreams unspoken, soaring high.

It swayed through storms, through gentle breeze,
It learned the art of moving with ease.

For even the wind that tried to break,
Was teaching strength with every shake.

It knew at last - it could not stay,
That endings too, have their own way.

So it let go - without a cry,
And found its peace in learning to fly.

And when it rests upon the ground,
Its journey's end makes life go 'round.

For every fall, each loss, each brief...
Begins anew — another leaf.

35. The last step

Though its fake and blur and Pain
Still, I wonder if I would be the main.

Facing and realizing every moment.
But do I do anything?

Performing everything till the end.
Results give me no stand!

Thats the last breath I took,
Which will not affect even the hook
Going through every possible look!

Getting, grabbing gambling the chance...
Was it just a mere glance?

Can't wait anymore..
It's already time.
Thinking about that every day.
But do I do that any day?

Trying to wake me up,
Till the last sup...

But Sad! I'm still stuck there
Who's gonna help me here,

The world is dark,
Can't even see a dog bark.

Can I leave this place please!
To Start Something new with peace...

And here's every moment I am trying... making it possible.

Have covered several miles,
The last step still remains
& remains & remains...

And here, our pages find their rest.
Every line was a thought shared, a feeling passed, a moment lived together. If these words brought you calm, courage, or simply a smile — then this journey has found its purpose.
Thank you for reading with heart.
May you carry a little of this story within you,
as you continue writing your own. ♥

— The End

www.ingramcontent.com/pod-product-compliance
Lightning Source LLC
Chambersburg PA
CBHW070458050426
42449CB00012B/3024